The Heart Is Where Love Is Born.

Table of contents

61. Goodbye my love
62. God embrace
63. She makes me sick
64. Lost love
65. Lovesong
66. I'm no superman
67. Saying goodbye
68. Mighty oak
69. I do not need to love
70. Streets of blood
71. Beyond my love
72. My love consume me
73. Moment to love
74 Love slave
75. Sweet embrace
76. Fallen night
77. Red, white and blue
78. Reflection of love
79. A good friend
80. A symphony to love
81. Strange love
82. A woman love
83. Broken wood
84. Intact loved
85. Sky dance
86. Whispers of love
87. Love unkind
88. Eternal love

Introduction

If you believe in love, love is the connection and happiness you feel toward someone. Love is the constant factors that help us to understand the meaning of love. I believe throw out the universe love is the same forces which determine the way we love each other.

Love is one of the driving factors which governed our hearts to fall in love. Love can be this powerful force which bound many people to fall in love. Like all other things, love has its opposite side to love.

However, love can be the force that can destroy with such a devastating outcome. I have seen the mighty fallen, because of a broken heart and cause many more to retread within their heart never to love again. When it comes to love, always remember love cannot change its properties or its element. It's only in the heart of the one you love is where love transformation of your feeling change love in it purse form to love or not to love

Dedication

    This book is dedicated to the special woman that will come into my life and share my love.

To love a woman is to dream
To dream is to love.
To truly capture the heart of a woman
Is to know the desires
Of that dream to be alive
And behold the wonders of the world.
So I say love and be loved
Only in the sweet bliss of a woman
You can know the desires of a woman heart.

Love is but a dream

Love appears then it's gone,
Like a fleeting dream, it can never overcome.
We came into this faded world
Apparently for some unknown scores,
The reason that we cannot comprehend the true meaning of love.
We lose ourselves in the one we love most,
With longing, we cannot give meaning to that love.
We feel the pain in our heart
And the emptiness in our soul.
We fall in love
With an empty dream,
Maybe with that special person
In a change for a better love
And we tell ourselves this is what love should be.
Is that what love is really about.
But then that same love is taken away,
So that what is left is
but an empty shell
Of a person to wander in darkness.
I will not stop loving
Until I find the true
meaning of love.

A second to fall in love

Let us make love, not in a moment
But in a second,
So love can bind our
Heart and soul with such emotional desire
Pleasing to the heart.

Let us count each touch
as we place gentle kisses upon
Our bodies with such love and desire,
Can express within the explosion bodies
Communication love without words.

Let us lay soft silence into love
For all others expression before making love,
Complementing the passion to please your
Soul mate in heart and soul in the ways of love.

Summer love

It is your soft love
That makes the rain to fall,
The sun to shine,
The flowers to smell so beautiful.
It is your tender love that makes
romance in summer,
Kisses in fall to feel the soft breeze of your love,
It is your love than I show
How to truly love you,
For you are my friend, lover, and love,
but most of all you are my wife.

Kissable love

It is that which
I long to hear.
Those soft sweeten words,
Comforting throw these kissable ears.
To remember sweet bliss,
making love in the hills,
Raindrops upon our skill,
Those lost moments,
The longing look upon your sweeten face,
From friends to lover
We love and play
But throw sweet love
It's our relationship remains the same.

The secrets of life

It is that love which blows
So tenderly in the misty reams of love.
So it may touch the very bounders to create life it itself.
Those souls that have to carry it ascents
Through life and death.
We see and feel it in
Our hearts that move
Us to care for each other,
But other times we turn
Our back on that same
Mist of life
And we dear to called
Ourselves human in the eyes of our creator.

Love throughout time

In this old house where my grandmother once live
There are these old stairs with character and love.
My mother used to tell me how her mother watch her play
Up and down those stairs with such fond memories
As her childhood turns into my son laughter.

As the years passed by an, I set in this old chair in this old house,
In taken back to my childhood with the laugher
Of my own children running up and down this old stairs cast
Full with the laughter of my grandmother in her youth.

But as time always past before our eyes
And laughter trap moments within itself,

I'm taken back to my mother smile
As the same smile is upon my face as
I watch my son sit in that old chair
And watch his children run up and down
That stairs case full with the character and love
Left behind by those that called this old house home.

Somebody

She is that somebody
That I must hold closely,
Kissing her soft sweet lips
Because of the femininity.
Her love is the storm that
Vanity beyond beauty,
Because she is that somebody
I must hold closely.
She carries her love
Tenderly inside her heart
And shower it with a need to be loved.
Her charm and beauty which
Carry her body like the white rose of fire,
That belongs to her tender soul,
That I must hold closely.

The direction of love

If you must fly
So open your wings
And let the wind
Take you to your true love.
But remember that the wind
Can change in any direction,
So kiss me goodbye,
Should you not return?
Or should I not be here
When you return for me.

Let it be

If it must be
So it should be
If it should be
So it must be

The great fall

If I should fall from this place
And my heart bush from my chest
I should close my eyes
And keep on falling
In the hope that this falling
Take away his outcall pain
In this silence I have
Made of my fallen life.
If I should fall from heaven
My only regret is that I have
Disobey my heavenly father in a moment
Of pride for someone else dilution
Of power.

Only for love

If I must love you
Let that be for love only.
Other men say here can offer you the world,
All I can offer you is love as one man to another woman.
Others may come with the gift of love
To keep your affection of lush and say
There love you.
Such the gift I offer none cannot
Compare to that of true love.
Other may say that they will love you forever
And forever and forever is a long time.
I can offer today and today only,
Tomorrow is the unknown story of love.
Others may kiss you then lies,
But the kisses I kiss are all from the heart,
So when I say let it be love only
So for love only I should
Say I love you.

A higher force

If I have learned that
Which propel my knowledge?
It is only because of my life
Have been touch by a
Greater force you may
Call God.

The sense of a woman

I whisper her name
It sounds so refine.
Such beautiful eyes upon a lady of light,
The true desire that captures mines.
Tears of women that
I last will echo.
Her love of beauty
Shinning beyond simple vanity of metal.
I have hunger so deeply,
I have smelled her sexuality,
But I must not deny
The senses of a beautiful woman.

Stone love

Oh, that should love thee
But not with a stone heart,
I have loved thee beyond heart and stones.
Thy stone love has travel
Into the darkness
Of thy love and found the bitterness of thy stone love.
I have pretended not to be a fool in your dream
But a man is all I am to fall in love with thee
And curse the heart the day I fall in love with thee.
Oh god,
Why have you stoned my hear with such a love
What if I should look upon a woman
My stone heart becomes a flesh
And I'm once a man again to feel the love of a woman.

I open my heart
And here you stand,
Not so beautiful, not so grand.
The brightness that once shines so beautifully
So dear is no more.
She stands by the light,
But her eyes are in darkness.
She once had beauty,
But it dies inside.
The fallen tears drop from her eyes,
Can never open the feeling
We once share so deeply inside,
To touch my cold heart.
You have lost that brightness,
So please forgive me
I do not love you anymore.

I must cry
Or I will die,
My heart has been
Curse with the sadness
And mistrusted.
I have lived my life
For only your caress,
Knowing that one day
I'm going to cry.
These tears in my eyes
And the sadness on my heart
It's tearing me apart
But I'm finding a new start.

My happiness

I may not put my emotions into love,
But my love for you my beloved
Is the strongest a man can love a woman?
And maybe I don't
Say enough to make my feeling clear to you,
But even so, I'm sure
You know that I love you,
my greatest happiness
In life is loving you.

My wife

I love you
For your trust in me
Your simplest smile I know
Is just for you
Because you love me so.
I love you for the way
You love me.
I love each moment
We both share,
I love you just knowing
That you are there
When love is needed,
But most of all
I love you for being my wife.

Funny girl

I know this girl
She is so funny
She makes me laugh
When I'm so lonely
I listen to her words
Such echoes whispers of true beauty
I know this girl
Who fulls me with beauty?
She such a lady
To keep that laughter
Full with the warmest of love
I know this girl
She is so funny
Sometimes I wish
She was my baby.

Back to love

As the crescent moonlight full night,
My life begins in more
Ways than one,
As I feel the life returning
To my broken soul.
There is a silence that hurt
So deeply in my heart.
Pain in the very soul
Of what it is to be human.
So I must take another love
To live throw another day,
So if you miss me in the day
I should be back to take other love
And love you once again.

Love upon my lips

As I contemplate the stern echoes in my soul.
The never-ending mysterious of shadows
Plaguing my emotions as I sit here,
Thinking about your sweet love.
This picture of you on the wall
Quicken my regret of lost love
Of these painful memories.
With each memory of you, it pains me in my soul,
To see you with another man.
For in my disappoints in love,
My only regret is that I could love you
When love was upon my lips
To say I love you.

New lover.

As the boney hand of death pass over my throne soul,
I can remember life as clearly as I took my first taste of love
With such happiness as
A moment's reflected in the tears that fall from these eyes.
I'm drowning in such pleasures
That comforts my every action
To the turn of my life in the
Motions of many forgotten lovers.
Those once happy moments resemble my life not to fade into the
night,
So I ask myself
Was life so hedonist that I drove my every
Action to turn out the lights
In the resemble of death?
What was once life is only distance light
Flicking of what I once was
Dislike in the joys of my life.
I was a fool to think that death was my only opinion
For a new life in other lover arms.

Shadow love

Call me my love
But let it be for love only.
My love is but a symbol
That stands for something,
It tormented me in terror of my own
Shadows of shame.
It gives me no pleasure or satisfaction,
But I carry the pain like a knife,
In my heart never to fade.
So what can I do?
It's a love in me; it's a love of mines,
Should I give up?
And bring shame to her that love me
Should I not live with that love?
Or lost the love of her that loves me back with her love.

Where love lives

So I must say goodbye to the simplest things which
Have capture my heart,
Knowing no more the special
Feeling I hope to tell you I love you.
This feeling consume each moment to tear my heart
From the very bondage that fights to keep us together.
We have fought a good battle, but our hate has
Capture that which we thought we could never lose,
So the fighting must stop and I must say goodbye.
So close your blue eyes and wash away the
Memories I have placed in your heart.
I cannot move where there is no space,
I always thought the time was our friend,
But I was wrong in the absents of love.

Summer love

It is your love that makes the rainfall to the earth.
The sun to shine,
The flowers to smell
And the birds to fly so gracefully.
It is your love that makes
Romance in the summer
And kisses in the fall.
It is your love that shows me
How to truly loved.
My wife, you are my friend, companion, and lover,
But most of all you are my life.

Forget us
When lives are long forgotten
And times have passed into the night
When moments fade into the next,
Which we can never escape from.
Forget us
When the love between
Heart and soul untangle
From a ream
Where true love cannot be undone.

Forget us
When men and women
live their life's
To grow olds into the next.

Forgot us
When you know more
And we can step from the shadows
And our lives have to begin

From only that moment
Our love for each other can only be remembered.

Forgot us
Only because you say we could not
Be in love in the eyes of those
That did not believe in true love
Of the heart and soul of true love.

Freedom

Feeling the air on my face
As freely as you can be
Life can change at any moment
So you must open up your
Mind and let it fly free.
A person must be free
To live among the stars
To fly far away
Just to be a shining star.

Falling

Dream of flying
In a sea of blue
Wings of silver
Could this be loved?
Stop, am falling, and am falling
Through a sea of blue
The wind holds me up
Like the embrace of a good
A woman likes you.
dreaming of falling
In a sea of blue
Eye's open, then lose
Dream of falling
Being not in love
Or in love with you,
Catch me in falling in love with you.

Obstacles to love

Oh come, my sweet love,
Come to my home.
These are the night that
Whisper our love.
It's the darkness that holds your hands
In a moment of comfort.
Your love is the fire that
Move upon the heart in
That beating of passion
Where space stop
And time being,
In that instant
Both of our love bound as one,
As there is life in
This heart of mines
Our love should pass
Overall fallen obstacles to come
In a moment of our whispers to love.

The meaning of love

Can you tell me the meaning to your love?
Is it the beating of my heart?
Or the beating of your soul?
Can you tell me the meaning to your love?
When it's not consumed to love,
Or in such moments compels to love.
Can you tell me the meaning to your love?
When our child look at me
And ask what the meaning to love.

Lovesickness

Can't you see am ill,
But the illness is not of the mind.
The heart has caught an infection
Which know treatment can cure,
Like an illness, it brought me pain
A never-ending heartache
Only loved can treat,
I have fallen in love
But love remains silent
To make an illness of my heart
To drive a man insane.

Love hurts

I cry for love,
I cry for pain,
The drop of my tears
Rundown my face.
What can I do?
What can I say?
My love was a dreamer
That wonders away
I wish I could stop her
But she moves like the wind,
The days pass by.
It became clear to me
It must have been a dream.
I will not cry because of the pain
I will not cry for love
But the beating of my heart
Brake all the same.

Time love

All I ever wanted is
To take your pain away,
With that love in your hear,
The fire in your eyes
You make me realize that
There is love in the world.
If I say that I love you
Will you believe a word I say?
But if I could travel throw time
There a lot that I will change,
You will be my only love
And I will take away your pain,
If I could travel throw time
I'll do it all for you
Only to have you in my arms
Just for one moment,
So to let you know
Your pain was mined to bear.

A simple smile

Her smile lights up my heart
Every time she enters the room,
At the time I wonder if it's me that
Brings on such a beautiful smile,
As I watch the dawn dance across
The distanced sky
As am drawn back to
Her beauty as she wakes up next to me
And she looks into my eyes,
At that moment I caught my own smile
In the reflection in her deep blue eyes
Smiling back at me.
Love can be a smile in the reflection
Of the one, you love looking back at you.

Lovechild

Her eyes as pearls
Most beautiful in the moonlight,
Her skin so tender
With the sweetness of daisies,
Upon the first sunset.
I try to capture the remnants of her loved,
Fallen moments,
A smile that is not so easily forgotten
Like the peddles in the wind,
So we love a little longer
And we love some more,
For in that moment of life
Which bloom in the air?
Growing roses,
The beating of our soul,
She began to wonder
Will it be a girl or a boy?

Lover or friends

Friends forever
Friends in the end
I know that I love you
And I'll know it in the end.
So open your heart
And Say it again
Should we be a lover?
Our friends in the end.

Lost love

I have loved
Two and to many,
But the heart is empty,
Without that somebody.
I have given all my love to,
But never to be returned,
Those were the ladies that
Could not fill me.
On the outside, I may look happy
But without true love
My heart consumes me,
I have walked alone
In the sadness of my heart
I may never know the true
Meaning of a women heart.

The proposal

Don't turn off the light my lover
I need to see how
Much you love me,
Look into my eyes
And let your love
Touch mines,
Don't say a word
Because of your eyes
Say all that is inside of me,
So let me say it for the
Both of us,
Will you marry me?

Dream lover

We dream of love
But we never follow out heart,
We set upon our love
As they pass us be like the
Raindrops from heaven.
We set around all-day
Wondering what to do,
When love is set upon your heart.
And the moment of love is set upon your heart
You must follow your desire
To the moment which
Will show you the
Dream of love
Which is in you to fall in love.

Shadows

Love walks away but doesn't cry,
My love is a storm deep inside,
Shadows of a ghost,
That walks the night
Looking for love all throughout the night.
For those who have love,
And see the light,
Are forever to walk the nigh
To see, but not blind,
For they should away be love
But only shadows, shadows
To remember love who haunt the night.

A moment to love

My heart walks the night looking for love,
Unable to find love and be a touch
By the magic, we call true love.
My heart and I don't know why
The lungless is always so deep in my soul.
I try to understand this feeling we call love
Only to have it slip away from me like a thief in the night.
Why can't I feel the love of a woman?
To enter my heart
And teach me about love.

The color of love

How did we go at this moment?
You and I here lying next to each other.
Did heaven open its gates?
And show us the way to love.
Did God speak the words?
And it became you and I
Entangle in the moment of love inevitable.
Falling from heaven,
Falling, falling,
Bless in perfection and the holy spirit
To become man and women.
Black and white entangle in a loving embrace,
Only to rise in the possibility
That love is not the color
God mad of lovers.

Expose

I love you heart
When you are sweet to me,
I love you lips
When you kiss me with a deep passion
Full with heavenly fires.
I love your eyes
With the warmness of each embrace entangle
With each glimmer, you cast upon me.
I love you words when you speak of love,
Full with each desire
To tell me you love me.
Oh, I stand at the bless of desire,
Calm hearted with virgin bliss,
And flamed joys
To tell you I love you.
Oh that my heart be fragile
And my love be pure,
For I stand before you in my
Virgin expose to show you
My love is true to you.

Love reborn

My love has died,
And I place it in my heart,
Where all of my broken dreams belong.
I place it next between heartache and heart-broken.
When I feeling sad I join them
And we talk about old times
When bitterness cloud our perception
About love and we laugh and cry
In our sorrow.

My love has died,
Like many dreams
To flash before my eyes
Of days to come knowing
That after the resting placed of love,
We will once rise again,
And have love reborn in our heart
To love again.

Let's be friends

How many times have I envy love,
To stand like a cold stone,
And walk in its darkness joyful love,
Only to have it flash before my eyes
In quick shameless goodbyes,
Only to envy it,
For am heartbroken.
Just once I will like to offer love,
But at last, am just the hands
Of broken dreams and lost love.
Oh, how I envy love,
To set next to me
And offer it friendship
So we can be friends.

Love promise.

If you were my lover,
I'll be your heart as the sun grace
The day with its rays of beauty.
I'll paint a masterpiece of your beauty
So the world can look upon you
As say there goes one stunting woman.
If you were my angel
I'll ask God for permission to marry you
So each time we send to earth
We will end up in each other arms and continual
Loving each other.
If you were my rainbow
Each rainy day your love
Will danced across the sky
Letting everyone know how much I love you.
If you were a love promise,
Each day loving you will be
Like living in a perfect moment of bliss.

Completeness

How can I make you understand?
How much you complete my life
And make me hold again.
I want you to understand
How special you are to me.
Before you came to my life
Each day fill me with such loneliness
You could never comprehend.
The moment you came into my life
You brought completeness
Which full every aspect of my being?
And offer me, love.
Your unconditional love makes me into
The man that stands before you
Asking for your hand of marriage.

Love reactions

Walking upon the grass
And feeling the lost in your heart
Of so many small moments.
The heart that has let stand
Still for too long
Never to capture the love lost.
We have a stand in the rain
And look up at the sky
And feeling the warmth drop of water
Falling upon your face
Only to be remember
The lost your heart feeling
For that which care for broken hearts?
We watch the leaves,
Feel from the tress,
So does your life come to beauty?
Sometimes we wonder why
Should we keep on for the reaction for love?

Love restores

May I kiss you?
Dusk restores me,
Behold I kiss them again,
I try to resist you.
You enter my heart and brought me, love.
You took my soul
Like a drowning man
Catching for his last breath of love,
If we should love
May I kiss your lips?
And let them restore me.

Family love

Love is a stranger
That most will say
It enters your heart
And take you away
It knows your name
With pain and tears
Mountains on fire
Two hearts on flames
It loves as a women
Comforting a man
Born as child
We shower it with love
With a feeling of joy
Hoping to bring us that
Special feeling inside
So the mountains may move
And the angels may cry
But with our love
Your heart will never die.

I miss you

My love,
The wind is blowing the winter leaves away
That falls to the cold earth,
The snow is falling
Like soft whispers in the night air of soul,
I see the rain washing away the snow
And the remains of me and you,
I feel so cold and the memories are
Not the same because you are not there,
Why did you have to stop loving me
And left me alone,
I miss you so much, my love.

Remember me

Remember me when wars are over
Remember me when we are not
In love any more,
Remember me when special moments
Are not there anymore to love you.
Remember the mere song of my heart,
Remember the way I kiss your lips,
Remember the way I hold your
Tender body with such compassion,
Remember me when my last days have come,
Remember me
Because I'll always remember you.

The music

Her body shines in the darkness
I want to play with her music
And created a harmonious rhythms
Of lovemaking between the two of us.
I urge her body to pick up such motion
To steady take deep breath
To say I love you.
I see her run not to touch the sky
And have raindrops
Wash away her teardrop when she cries
Because tension brake her heart to say
I love you.
I watch her look upon our child
And take a deep breath
Then look at me and say
How happy I may
To create a harmonious song with you.

Dream lover

I'm so lonely and empty inside,
I don't want to be alone anymore,
I look upon my lonely heart
Wondering why can I find true love,
Each time I see your beautiful face
My heart jumps a beat
And sink back a million miles
Waiting to tell you I love you.
Each night as I lay my head to sleep
I dream of you,
I can't wait to close my eyes
So I can have a perfect love
But even my dreams betray me.
I plague with thoughts kissing and holding you,
But I know my loneliness
Will not leave me alone
Because each night I lay my head to rest
I dream an imperfect dream of you
And that makes me feel empty inside
When I open my eyes
Knowing I can never have you.

An open heart

How could I be so in love?
In a heart, I know too well
How could I be so happy?
Knowing that you love me so much.
We are finally together
Knowing that we can never part,
You surround my heart with so much love
I will never be lonely again,
How could I be so happy?
Because I'm surrounded by your beauty.
I'm in a heart I know so well.

My master

Loving you is my master,
You control my every emotion,
The first time I saw you
I became a fool in love
And a victim of your beauty.
You took over my life with just a word.
I have become someone I love to be around
Because you have become my master.
Thanks to my love
You have given me a life
To have dreams and goals
To direct my life to love you.
I can never see my life without
Because you have become that
the master who loves me.

The meaning of love

Thought out the years
We have loved each other
In the blink of a lifetime,
There were moments
When we struggle
To keep the relationship
From tearing us apart,
But in moments of sadness and heartbreak
The only thing that keeps us together
Was knowing
The things we one hold important
Did not matter know how much we love each other?
We love each other
And still found time to what really matters
In our life's to keep on loving each other.
Now that our love has grown old
And we along with it
We can still smile at each other
And remember why we love each other.
Love is not how much time you love the other person
But why understanding why
You fall in love with that person.

Goodbye my love

As I set and read this letter
My heart breaks in a million pieces,
The letter read, my dear love
The pain I feel hurt so bad right now,
I know we can never be together again
So I want to say I have always loved you,
Please don't come and look for me
Because you will never find me.
Do not worry about me anymore
For I'm not alone anymore,
I have found a blissful peace
I have been looking for all my life,
Please do not think I have forsaken our love
That is the farthest thing from my mind,
I must say goodbye and I love you
And will miss you
Because death has captured my eyes
And God told me to say goodbye
To my only love.
Please don't cry
I only wanted to say goodbye my love.

God embrace

If you see my love
Tell her I'm looking for her,
She will be the one that looks like a beautiful painting,
Her uniqueness is one of a kind,
In a room full of a beautiful woman
She will be the prettiest one with the biggest smile and eyes,
Her angelic beauty makes her feel like she needs wings
To keep her heaven-bound.

If you see my love
Tell her I'm looking for her
Because if you found her
Ask he will she love me where
Angel wings twinkle in my eyes
She is God most beautiful, angel
And I ask her to come home
To god embrace where she belongs.

She makes me sick

She makes me sick
With every desire in the soul
I curse the day that my eyes fell upon her beauty,
She was that girl
I thought I could hold closely
When the fire was cold as ice,
I look into her rose blue eyes and the dames
Of emotions fume throw every though
I recalled of her love.
She makes me sick
But through it all, I love her cruelly.

Lost love

She moves like a swan
With grace in the form
Morning falling snow
In the era of her birth,
She walks on the wind with
Her wings in motions,
Her love is a dancer
That ace for the storm
She may not know my name
Our the feeling I share
But she will always be
That love which I let walk away
Because there was some about you
I could not love you.

Lovesong

She sang me a song
A song of beauty
The words were of love
And the best of honey
It was a lofty tale of
Two lovers making sweet love,
It enters my heart
And make me insane,
So love your sweetheart
Without pain,
Sing her a song of the time
That wonders away,
Trying to hold on to that specials day,
So look into her eyes
And touch her sweetly
Saying those words
That makes her feel lovely
I do love you with love
Song of a million songs
For once in a lifetime
She sang me a song
Of true love bayou beauty.

I'm no superman

He walks like the wing
With love and fetish
Full of beauty and love like no other
My heart has been
With the warmest and thunders
I love my pretty
But she thinks I'm a mess
I live in the bushes
And I make know the arrest
I fight for freedom
Then I get some rest
I have traveled the world
And cross the sky
I'm not superman
I'm just a guy
With love upon my chest,

Saying goodbye

So I must say goodbye
To the simplest things
Which have to capture my heart
Knowing no more to raptures
The special feeling I hope to tell you I love you
This feel I consume me at this moment
Is tearing my heart from the bondage
That fights to keep us together,
We have fought a good battle
But our hate has capture
That which we thought we could never lose,
So the fighting must stop
And I must say goodbye,
So close your rose blue eyes
And wash away the memories
I have a place in your heart,
I cannot move where there is no space,
I always thought the time was my friend
But I was wrong in the eyes of love
So please forgive me when you close your eyes
And try to wish away the love
I hold for you,
So I must say goodbye
When you love someone.

Mighty oak

Stay tall and mighty
And still, be young
Like the flowers so tender
They soon will be gone.
For years I stand to comfort you
Watching you grow
With the mightiest of hands
The day is upon me
But still, I stand strong
There cutting my forest down
With the quickest of hands
Stay strong and mighty
And still, be young
Once a mighty oak
Topple to the grown.

.

I do not need to be loved

Step beyond steps
But nowhere have they led me
Shadow in shadows
A place in reality
But no one to find me
I'm drowning in forever
And wishing for a reality
Without a lover
Love comfort me
So love me or hate me
But please do not shadow me
For in this world
I do not end to be love.

Streets of blood

Street of blood
Mothers go running
Children nowhere
To be found
Father on drugs
What can I do?
I'm just a child
Please love me
Without streets of blood.

Beyond my love

Take my simple heart
And do with it as you wish
Take my joyful dreams
And do with them as you please,
For in the eyes of love
I accept the sacrifice,
I cross the longest deserts
Just to be with you my love
In days and night
I have opened my torched soul
In sunshine and darkness
Just to feel what is to be loved by you,
I should love you better and beyond
Into my life and better after my death.

My love consume me

My love, you came into my life
Like the beating of my heart
She consumes my thoughts
To love in a way
I could never comprehend,
She is that love which
Open all doors
To my soul and heart
Which makes me feel sad in a way
Because my love consume all that I am
Love or be consumed?
From the beating of my heart
And the love which she offers
I have only but one choice
For in my need to be loved
My heart should be forever
The burning of passion
For she that consume me.

A moment to love

My love soft eyes pierce my soul with
A look that sank me to the
The very depth of unspoken desire,
Her is a love that touches my will
To love in a way that I
Tough was impossible to feel,
I have a look into the pools
Of her rose blue eyes and saw the love
She offers to me,
I can't deny these feeling
I have for her,
Can this be the end of the beginning?
To the desire, I have found
A new Place in my soul to Rome for my love.

Love slave

Please tell me what to do my love
Cause I'm obsessing about you,
I'm always walking away
Please tell me what I must say
Cause I'm devoted to you,
My every breath is but an echo
Upon the wind
Because of your love
Have made a slave of me.

Sweet embrace

The desire of your sweet passion
Capture the ripe of my love,
Such is the love which
Compels my every passion
Which cannot depart
From this torched heart,
All I wish for is your sweet embrace
And the tenderness of
Your forbidden heart
Beating next to my heart,
Oh my love
The mere song of your soulful heart,
In my sweet embrace which gives me
The desire of wanting
Your love with a deep rapture
I cannot control for you
I'm wishing that our romance
Will be that love which lasts a time
In that moment of true love.

Fallen night

The distance stars
That rise brightly in the sky
The crescent moon had
Set upon the forgotten night.
The darkness that surrounds the
Mist in life can never compare to her love.
The fallen night
The night not so bright
Have taken my love
Like knowing whispers
Echo to the night
Oh that I have loved her
And love not of her,
The fallen night
Have taken my love of thee.

Red, white and blue

The dream was a dreamer
Of hope and high
Hoping for freedom
To glide her eyes
She shows us the love so deep and true
For pride and glory
Red and blue
We remember her life
Legacies and tides
Dreaming of dreams
We must not close our eyes
But show and try
That the dreamer of a life
Reflected in the reds and blues
Which we fly so high
The dreamer was a dreamer
Of so many lives
For the red, white and blue.

Reflections of love

The fires which burn like
Running waters
Consuming the reflections
In the midst of life
Deeping the soul
To destroy the myths that
Full our imagination to see
The reality in the reflections
Which consumes the heart and soul
Of a love not taken to be love.

A good fiend

The passing of a good friend
Is not an easy thing to comprehend?
The situation becomes even harder
When you truly love that person
With deep love in your soul.

Oh take away this pain
My love, so I can feel not love
But of deep sorrow taken from a love

The passing for a close lover
Tears at the heart
Like knives in the heart
With no relief in sight
As I sit here with a river
Running from my eyes

It's with a heavy heart
That I try to bring some
Comfort to my soul for her that I love
But why did my friend, lover, and wife had to die

The passing of a good friend
Is never easy to comprehend
When taken from love.

Symphony of love

Oh night be full with the scornful pain
As the wind dance across ghostly pones
You could hear sexuality of echoes
Being play out as creation comes to life
The moon cast its reflections upon
The murky waters as each echo brought
A delightful romance
That beckons for creation
In that murky pone
As each frog echo
A symphony to love.

Strange love

My life is a stranger
Which pass and beckon to be love?
In this mad, mad world
What I'm I to do
Stop, stop, and stop
My mind cannot stand it any longer
Please leave me alone to love
I have lost my lust to love again.

A woman love

The sea cries the deepest tears
Within the sea less bluest heart
A woman cries the bluest cries
For the love
She may never soften her heart
The heart of a lover
The tender touch of a woman
A cry with known compassion
The heart of a woman
Cries the deepest tears
For a love more sweeter than
The heart of a woman love.

Broken wood

As the cold sun came into the broken window
Like a newly sunrise of soft flower
Love could smell the poorness
In the house
She could hear the voice
Of mother in the small room
Where wood should be burning
There was none and she feels the
The sadness of the mother-heart with her
Every breath for life.
Love could see the pain in the mother's eyes
As she walks toward mother
Loves feel the coldness
When she asked the mother what was wrong
There were no words
But she could tell
There was no food to eat
Because there was know
Fire to warm the house.

Intact heart

The years have been long
But my soul has remained intact
As a man, I have to walk a fine line
Between love and passion
I have tasted the forbidden fruit of desire
And it blooms in my heart
Like forgotten passion.

The years have been long
And it's time for me to rest
I must put away the toys of my youth
And remember the joy my manhood
For at the end of my journeys
It was my heart which stops me
From becoming a lonely man.

The years have been long
But my wife and kid
Have given me the heart
To continual loving as a father and husband.

Sky dance

They dance upon the wind
In all forms of shapes
They bring us happiness
In the moonlight and the rain
For we call them by name
But what there are
We may never know
They move as ships
In the storms like a lonely soul
The night passing into days
But they stay the same
Sky to sky
We look at the blue and we
Say that we know not of them
From day today
They dance across the sky
Dancing a dance of love.

Whispers of love

There is no end to the
Love that has entered my life
I have observed the stars every night
But the people I have loved
Fade into the unspoken moment to
Whisper no more to the night
I Traveling to a place where
Joy is pleasurable and love is forever
Someday my love will come again
And I will move on to love
But until that day
I will carry on loving
Which has never faded?
And not forgotten in my heart to love you.

Love unkind

These moments of time
There passing us by
Our fading memories
Lost secrets in time
Candles in the windows to lead you
Toward my heart
Forever beating your soul to us depart
I remember such moments
When our love entrains
Like lusty lovers
One moment define
Do you not love me?
And those loves define
But you are asking for a divorce
And that is unkind.

Eternal love

I will die for her
With body and soul
Sweet love, I adore her
Oh heaven me more
A body of botchily
And the face of a goddess
Such a heaven creature
An angel I adore

I will live for her love
Which capture my soul?
A lasting aroma
With just one kiss
She tangles the lips of a rose

To die without her love
Is to know such pain
But to live with that love
Is to comfort that eternal love.

True friendship

A true friendship that span
Space and time
One bound that share a hand with mines
Tick tock in motion
A true friendship it extends
Throw the fabric of time
One moment in reality
One moment in time
A true friendship between
A Husband and wife.

In love embrace

Trying to compare roses in spring
Kisses in the dark
Walks in the park
To the touch of the woman I love
Is like being in heaven

You can offer me the world
Or the stars in the heaven
But the love she offers me
None can compare

To love my woman
Is like taking a
Bath in love
From birth to death.

Open storm

Walking upon the brown grass
And feeling the bitter pain in your heart
Of so many small broken soul's
That has let stand
Never to recapture such moment,
We have stood in the rain
And look upon the sky and feel
The warm drops of tears drops
Falling to your face only to remember the lost
Your heart feels,
For that which you care for
We watch the leaves
Fall from the trees
And your life comes to an end.
Sometimes we wonder why
Should we keep on with the reason for life?
The most of life we can recall
Are the sad parts
Which bring no comfort in a broken heart?
But we still move forward in the hope
That life is but a clam storm taken
From the heart.

She

She makes me sick
But I love you only
She gives me pain
She gives me love
She gives me her heart
And the stars above
Her love as honey
The pains so sweet
She is my lover
And I love her truly

Broken love

You say that you love
With a deep passion
Taken from the lips of God,
That's what it came to be,
I was a brave man
With fire and flames,
Noting could enter because I was not the same,
You broke my soul
With the same passion
You say that will not change and
That's was the reason not to
Fall in love again

Quacking of love

You make me smile
With the quacking of love
The warmth of your heart
And the comfort of your soul.
The smell of your sweetness
Like the flowers of May,
The touching of your body
To the quacking of May,
We walk hands in hands
To this very day
To the quacking of sweet love
Such days of May.

Love remain

Running through golden flowers
Hearts beating of love
The smell of roses and the stars above
Hands in hands
Only she can tell
Am I her love?
Only love can tell.
Hearts beating of fire
Water running from wells
Our love has travel
And touch each cell,
Moving our body into our minds
We have moved so far
But our bodies remind full with life,
Our hearts, onc life
Until the day you call me your lover.

Snowflakes

You love is the rainbow
That falls to your face
Like running snowflakes.
It comes as pain.
If we are one
And must illuminate the same
Say that you love me
And make the pain goes away.

A different kind of love

So many of us look at love as a
Exclusive emotion
A man loving a woman,
But as many of us can see
Love can take many forms
Of many kinds
Man loving man
Woman loving woman,
When a person alls in love
It's the happiness time
Of their life's
But when a person
Love the some sex
They get cast out for being in love
We must learn to accept a person
For what they are
A person of love and deep emotional feeling.

Please leave

What is a man without love?
What is a day without a night?
You enter my life
And destroy my dreams
Into my mind and wash away my memories
You say that you love me
But then you walk away
Leaving me standing at the edge of heart brokenness
And lost forgotten dreams,
What am I to do?
Love you or not to love you
With a sweet kiss
You say goodbye and leave
I wish you could have a stay
So you could see true love in me.

When I love you
Let it be for love only
Do not take my love
How it seems to be
But for what I have to offer
In the form of love.
If my love should cause you pain
Then my purpose has no
Meaning in your eyes
Of the one that loves you
So look upon my love
And recall with loving memories
What we once share
For only in that state of love
You have given meaning
To call me your lover and friend,
But if you believe you heart
Could not understand my love
When you leave just remember
I should love you to the end.

Forgive me

When you see that I call no
More for your love
It's not that I do not love you anymore,

When you see that know more roses arrive
As your open door
With a special not saying I love you
Do not think my love has gone away,

When you sit by the cell phone
And waiting for my call
Please don't be mad if I do not call,

But most of all, please
Do not be sad when the police
Knock on our door
And tell you I have lost my life,

Please forgive me, my love
I was on my way home
To tell you I love you.

A million kisses

I can feel your love upon my face
As I enter through the door of our house,
The memories of you love to welcome me
Like a lost friend you have not seen in years,
Love gone but not forgotten
Waiting here beyond that close door,
As I enter the door you warm arms embrace me
With the look of amazement in your eyes
As you jump upon me
And began to bath me in a million kisses,

Remember me

Remember me when
You hear that I'm no more,
Remember m when you called
My name I do not respond,
Remember me when God
Tell me to come home
And I could not say goodbye,
Remember me, my love
Because when I close my eyes
The only person I will
Remember is you, my love.

Wondering soul

As your love set in my heart
I wonder where you are,
As the heavenly bodies dance across the sky
I wonder if you still love me tonight,
I'm just a wandering soul
Looking for your love tonight,
In a galaxy full with life
I leave this world
Without telling you goodbye,
I can never comprehend why I had to die
And leave my love behind,
Each night as the stars shot across the sky
I wish upon the night
To be there with you,
Each time my heart stands still
I can feel your love
Like a million sun about to set,
I hope when I see god
I will ask him please don't let you cry.

Love forever

I just wish I could love you forever,
let the world finally share in our love,

I'm can never get tired of loving you;
I still feel the love in my heart

I love the fact that you still love me
each and every day,

through the hard times and the good
You remain by my side
Refusing to give up on me.

If I could love you forever
I only wish to show you my true feeling,
my head might stop its constant beating
To tell you I love you.

Bio

My name junior Griffith and I'm a writer and painter. My works writing or painting show deep aspects of my life which have a profound impact on my creative thoughts to write or paint. Many believe art has no relevance; however, I find myself continually returning to those aspects which create the hidden or misrepresented in the world we live in and my diverse approaches to making art. When the images are painted on canvas or word is put on paper it charges it a reality so that when the image changes, it leaves a trace of the image before it, often affecting the image which comes next, in a way that art evokes everything for us.

My art education has been a self-taught one. My early career in abstract construction and later psychology degree and poetry has provided an interesting combination of visual aesthetics and human psychology. My detailed and colorful abstract painting is filled with layers of rendering from my poetry, revealing the ambiguity that exists in every individual thing and the setting that makes that individual thing come alive. I consider myself a Human Realist, my work conveys the colorful experience of "the face in the motion of life", playing music, writing poetry and often in leisure, posing in front of a camera. Growing up in the late eighties and experiencing the surge of a music revolution which influenced me greatly and has allowed me to paint a musical symphony or recite the poetry of my formative years. My every motion has its own unique map and conveys a sense of depth captured best with paint and poetry. Not only does the world color provide a fascinating landscape to explore, My aims at capturing what's beneath the surface, particularly the mysteriousness of the world motion and often the energy they embody it help me to create my life and the art paintings of poetry, I love to create in form and motion in which I celebrates the world around me in colors and words..